BLOOD LORD

By Hugh Seidman

COLLECTING EVIDENCE

BLOOD LORD

BLOOD LORD

Hugh Seidman

DOUBLEDAY & COMPANY, INC.
GARDEN CITY, NEW YORK
1974

The original versions of some of these poems first appeared in publications:

"Blood," "Blood Lord," in *Seneca Review,* Copyright © Hobart & William Smith Student Assn., 1973; "California," "Out Take," in *Ploughshares,* © 1972 by Ploughshares, Inc.; "As the Sea Saves," "The Bus Treads 10th," "Muse," in *Mulberry,* Copyright © 1972, Mulberry Press; "Refusing the Oath," in *Mulberry,* Copyright © 1973, Mulberry Press; "Hunting Bormann," "Finding the Felt," in *Equal Time,* Copyright © 1972 by the Equal Time Press; "From the Heights," in *Ant's Forefoot,* reprinted by permission; "The Bracelet," in *Choice,* all rights reserved by Choice Magazine, Inc., Copyright © 1972; "The Great Nebula in Andromeda," in *Antaeus,* © 1973 by Antaeus; "The Muse," in *Westbeth Poets,* Copyright © 1971 by Westbeth Corporation; "Veblen & Ellen," in *Harper's;* "Loving Women," in *Harrison Street Review,* Copyright © 1972, the Harrison Street Review; "Drop the Wires," in *The Nation,* Copyright © 1970 by the Nation Associates, Inc.; "Aubade," in *The Nation,* Copyright © 1973 by the Nation Associates, Inc.; "Death, Which Is," in *New American Review;* "Greene Street," in *Unmuzzled Ox,* Copyright © 1971, Michael Andre; "The Last or the First," "Screen Dream," in *Unmuzzled Ox,* Copyright © 1973, Michael Andre; "At the Pole," "Of the Plane," in *Salmagundi,* Copyright © 1971 by Skidmore College; "Under the Floor," in *Caterpillar,* Copyright © 1970 by Clayton Eshleman; "Vermont," in *Caterpillar,* Copyright © 1971 by Clayton Eshleman; "Story," in *Pot-Hooks & Hangers,* Copyright © 1973, Pot-Hooks & Hangers; "Untowards," in *New York Quarterly,* Copyright © 1972 by the New York Quarterly; "Poem," in *Penumbra,* reprinted by permission.

Acknowledgment is also made to the New York State Council on the Arts (Creative Artists Public Service Program) and to the National Endowment for the Arts for their assistance, and to the Yaddo Corporation for a period of residence, during the time in which some of these poems were written.

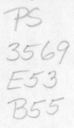

ISBN: 0-385-08172-3 Trade
0-385-08173-1 Paperbound
Library of Congress Catalog Card Number 73–10546

CONTENTS

7

BLOOD LORD

SECTION 1

BLOOD

At one time I thought
I will come thru this at one time
with my mind I thought
I will come thru this as I came
from the pitch-hole of doll men
to each I had loved
embraced on the sea's plain
as the sun blazed
resurrection as with Susan when I said
you are how the dream was but *We*
are the blood volley's
craft of transfusion
for the robots draining blood
who know what their bodies know
of the black crusted blood words
that leak as our hearts leak
when the language stops

I wish I could write you
that joy cooing *dada*

in lucite air with the rifle's puff smoke
but I am bound to my blood
in the life which is as mad as blood
unturned in revolution
from the jargon of your body
the Patriarch's double spy
the wrong key
to break their secret code

CALIFORNIA

Murder and no names
for the excitement of law that the ax cuts
my own genitals to butcher her. America
sucked on its fuse.
The days congealed. The heights
of billions of years burned in information,
I did not want prose
tho the poem could do no more
for the Laurel Canyon Road with Deanna
and her actor, in karate
on the Sunset Strip, in Venice
or on Noe Street. Laurie
forgot she had forgotten me.
At Big Sur
Miranda walked. The sea lions
barked on the rock skin.
It was not then the outward sun
but the night of inattention

without image but itself to prove
how can we change or how
can we not be changed misery
loving insufficient knowledge.

OUT TAKE

It was time to splinter doors.
The stairs of water.
Blood running from a light bulb.
A gun dreaming of a glove.

How does a pregnant woman plead for her life?
He shut the book.
The night was disabling itself or
He opened the book—to deal
Upon the vengeance of the Lord.

Literature, the Lüger.
Read and be dead. Tho mountain
At the semblance of the light.
The dynamite in the phone.
The birds taking part.
Gouged out her eyes it said.

Master,
You saw the rose but

Who are these forms
Accusing us,
No matter what,
We are insane.

And the films made and
The heads beheaded and
The Real Thing.

REFUSING THE OATH

In Christ's guilt, in spite
I argued agony to break
archetype's vice
money to live, forceps
as nitrate
burns newborn eyes, skin slit
to its vile screech

All males are cut, the uncut
is not natural, women know
birth is hate
it was a child's place
in the breath as State
the hospital's spattered tiles
mapped clearly our pus
she was a stranger and pregnant
she had clap and I drove
the whine of a climax
thru her walls

Ejaculate murderer yet not at peace
head's hate of pelvis
chin's rage and clenched fear
the sewers of complexity, complexity
like galaxies'
black holes, intelligence
that we are, the thin bones
eaten in the blood, universe's
shift to the red
infinite, lip-close

HUNTING BORMANN

So that altered and the same
we came at where Bormann was
myself, and the assassins, for the pig
as it pleased him, to be known
as in his joke—
alive in Argentina

The rain fell in torrential reprisal
it is art, my friends
to render this farce believable
it is named the enormous tomb
where brought on my birthdate
Bormann instructed us
and the video-freaks
who caught him for the tube
as their women had demanded
for the pureness of my day
on my knees, stroking air, pretending
your hair has been shaved
it is awful to love you this way

it is not my fault
but I pay for you, for Bormann
for the perfection of these women
for whom nothing can be done

It is August 1st
and the casting is timed
for the corpses of the crowd
and later on the tape the white
light that cannot be explained
tho the Yugoslavs had lost 4
and the Poles 2 and tho
my people were at war
in an endless loop I knew
that I was to be the first casualty
in his instant replay for the fans

BLOOD LORD

Who was it banged on the window
emptied of dream, Blood Lord
I may speak it now
Blood Lord
his fingers are ropes, his heart
the long sought
perpetual machine, entropy zero, here
for we who have withheld

Last night
the color TV spanned pleasure
guerrillas butchering cream
the latest whores and pimps
revising metaphysics
we were both on the great triple bed
were reclining at apocalypse like kings
enlightenment on all channels
guavas and *pineapples*
shitty little Christ fruit
spitting needles thru the meat

25

of 3 year olds on the Stone Age
Plain of Jars, corpses
on scanning scopes
in the air-conditioned cockpits
reconnaissance helicopters
automatic gun ships and bombers

There have been many subtle themes on this theme
the banality of shadows
shut from their sun
this is the boredom of history
but we sleep as the credits come
with a last kiss, a last
twisted dial to miss
nothing as we have not of our true work
our hands scouring sky to press us to
the sill's soot, the blue
edge where murderers pause
before paradise, the recoil
as the cab halts or the elevators
fall so that millions
are assured and are sure again
that when the day is cleared
his switchblade will be pure
and will redeem them

POEM IN FAVOR OF THE WAR

Women and the men, the guilty, who have hold
who are planed into my anger who postulate
penitence that I hate
in my allegiance to the martyrs who deserve
to take violence, that nobility
the dead lend to their hands
for forgiveness and I give them
the forgiveness of the gun

I had wanted the murder to be over
but by compassion I became
the maniac of murder
and each day as on all days
I have argued in anguish—it is true
that they beg, that the mind is pain
the ploughshare beaten back to sword
I know this is anger on the astral
I know but I am worthy now to know
I am worthy of what before me
was filth in their butchership

27

And I come to it having broken it
and I deal it as the sea
deals its orders for the armies
turning ardor to the blood wheel
and now I am for all crime and you
who are the platitudes, the X's
of morality, the geniuses of anus
it is I who drive entropy
it is I who leave no heart, it is I
who grind the armaments the stars offer
to a seeker after vengeance

And now it is my time for redemption
as the body times spew for the cleansing
when the mothers jam a son to the nail
and the roses plead
adornment by the thorn
in their deaf art marking sentence
and as the sun burns, I mock and burn
and as the branch fans, I am wind
and as the child and the lovers lust, I love
and as the book is signed, I sign
I, Of Butchering
and as the Christ found, I have found
the continent and the blood river
holy unto butchering

SECTION 2

FROM THE HEIGHTS

Susan
I rode those days from class
my father the driver
hands clutched to the wheel in rigid control
buildings that they send in the post cards
boats to Brooklyn Mailer's house
Zukofsky around the corner
years ago Whitman my old school on Jay Street
Ginsberg and the little mouse that weeps in the cat hole
be kind to yourself Hugh he says

Bearing the body thru each of the hours over black water
and then the morning sun blazing on the windows
when I came and came out of you and thought
it burned there because of love
the blaring horns crying
for the sorrow I have lived in
holding back everything and everything
profoundly breaking the tears to mirror
the way that they are and are necessary
to be free of this vice that locked me

The baby picture boy you carried on your breast
what I could not have done child's hand
reaching to touch a face be near his mother
sniffing coke in the polluted sky of the morning sniffing
junk in the polished sky of the morning when the light
went on and on

THE BRACELET

The bracelet of sixteen stones put by you
at the pulse of my wrist in color the earth has worked
is a puzzle to myself who have always
mistrusted adornment and color and have dressed
in the coldness of the sky and sea
for I have bought shirts and scarfs of
lavenders and yellows and a pair of salmon corduroys
with red and brown shoes and have placed
a gold rug in my bathroom and a larger rug
of deep and brilliant reds at the floor beneath
three windows where the north light comes
to a white and yellow plastic table and these things
are a wonder to me as are you who have brought this upon me
like an amazing reimbursement of the spring

NEWTON

Newton, praise Newton, his tree
the apple is free

Newton praises diaphragm and foam
blood cotton, twisted tampon
the equations of motion are worked and do

Sink of underclothes
thigh thru hose, armpit and moon
the *bi*nomial theorem is proved

Newton anoints with vaseline and gell
he blesses the stretch mark
3-body problems are done in his bed

Nipple hairs tickle Newton's nose
he feasts on cheese of toe, he cries
Hosanna to the head

Newton meditates the wheel
tantrik of navel, mandala
he feels on the calculus of skin

Newton says yes to the douche
to the tweezed brow that curls
he loves the gush and breath

The pot of leg wax and the bleach
are his alembic and alchemy
his come is the coin of his mint

Newton bears witness to tongue
blood, buttock, cunt and smell

Newton rides the planet's flow
heaven and hole, comet tailed
lucky and wonderful, blissful Newton

THE GREAT NEBULA IN ANDROMEDA

That woman, vacuum in her mouth
arms extended, the stars
budding in her entrails
the last invasion
the ship's gantry gently
cracking in the windows
the alien secret of the breath
as the spine is kissed
and the serpent stirs
the sense of the infant's eyes
alive with light
and the women who have sung
of the silk dripping cunt

This is the hour when history starts
when the nipples are sucked
between my lips
and the Buddha winks and presses
his mouth to mine
in memory of the past

36

that he was confounded by
at the rim of the universe
when sight turns back
to the center of all things and this
my darling, my incredible angel
is the silence and the noise
I taste and know nothing of
gripping at my ears

AUTIST

For Frances

Already the mind, struggling to reform
struggling to reconceive its indifference

At Florida where the world had turned
to the height of an unalterable sun
the mind might have wondered at this stratagem
omniscient in the choices of effect and cause

That sun among the millions
reinstructed in the contours of the mind
and the light, consumed in alteration
to plunge the mind thru more

The way bodies had touched as the mind
reconstructed their distortions real enough
for the scrutinies of a mind

He meant, it should have been done and it was not
as if the bullet had jammed in the gun
or the drowned left buoyed upon the wave

38

At Florida he had believed in that sun
and the changes that even a mind might not alter
and yet, performs in the unrecoverable
arisen daily and hung to imitate the day

THE MUSE

You were the liar,
stabbing your needle to be free.

It was your reason above the laurels
and it was the only reason
you did not tell
until the end
when there was no reason
to tell of anything.

There are the silent worlds
we touch invisibly.
You saw your father in the stone and passed him by.

Not even this will fade,
not even now
would you alter your refusal.

This is what they meant when they said
forgiveness;
Or the moon that groans with veins.

40

Your wish was always for control,
always for the human god
and always
you were the mad woman
raging thru your eyelids for the bone.

Where they came for you, like snow,
those moths that burn
fixed on an instant and its splendor.

FINDING THE FELT

For Stephanie

Taut body's breast curve and back
of thousands of photographs look at me
shaking with anger

where you were or
you were
no where

had come from the bookstore
had had peace for a time but could not
enter this hymn to you

against the contraction of organs
of the brain itself
the putrid lips and intestines
of you in your death dream
Akutagawa's
rotted apricots

and my hate
at the paintings of your walls
that could buy me my life

How many times the stomach clench
as Freud had smoked
endless cigars the fear fact of cancer when
he would not take drugs and that this rage
was told me as virtue

that pain is unreal
that pain is real but the feeling of it unreal
that I have not felt the pain and therefore feel pain

You were the muse whom I begged for sleep
the courtesan deceiving me with oil
the immense eyed child

you felt my power and made it
the aloneness of inequity
that became the world
so that I knew myself
the outcast from what we were

to come to the women whom you kissed
to erection of the man I was
and not the small son

I pounded the hardness you softened
only for these sisters

imponderable mystery
whose desire the iron followed to the magnet's answer
that you were a woman and resisted
the perfections of what had never been
to remain yourself

as when we went on the black hill thru unnatural
blueness and the stars
where you had held me in
the beat and the maze of such clockwork

to awake to the canvases
in payment for your different blueness

where the oddity of my hand in yours or the fire
of the nightmare's talk
was approaching a finality of which
even such an art might be envious

VEBLEN & ELLEN

The beatific swimmer's face
glistening in the lake
the paint-like lawns
thru the green glass as if wet
the power of the pianist after dinner
he was hunting her again
in the compromise flesh makes
he was singing as the car flashed
with 3 coming fast

He was striking it at last
as his mother had hoped
on the piano at 8
delivered as the kids jeered
the faggot who would play
for now he had its key
he was cold at its teeth
he shivered as he had seen her
that morning in Minnesota
on the winter Mississippi
out of Brooklyn of the dead

45

She was Ellen Rolfe
Great Northern's daughter
theosophist blue stocking
niece of the Carleton College
6 months Veblen's wife
on the river to pick plants
a child's sex organs
when they opened her
numinous as Northfield
where the James gang
hit the bank in '76
and Thorstein walked
from his father's plow
to green Yale and Kant

In fantasy land
there is a love song
called *The First*
it was his now he has wrung it
from the swimmer in the light
from the sickness of her hurt
from her callow breasts
attempting to be adequate
from her body at the airport
frantic to find him it is done
as the water off the car wheels
at 80 slapping windshields
as those women passed

THE PURPLE HAZE

The clear-eyed, baby-faced
peaceful priest dealer
from the mountains
on Fifth & 8th

Are you a cop, he asks
and do I know the streets or where to sell

But in a store
I meet you with the man you love
and weeks before, the hip young businessmen
who glean upon the world

The pressure starts
and nothing lets it go

A woman there was reading palms
and I kept thinking how
I should get back to work
to write this out, to read to you

The pressure starts
and nothing lets it go

They make a $100,000; more
I left

The problem was the hole
that nothing fills
and yes, you've heard that one before

I closed the door and up the street
I looked to see the windows where
you always used to live

It's alright, isn't it, I mean
whatever's done is done

But actually this is
Pavese's poem
he called you Constance then

What women in their weakness do
it took humility
not pride
and now he'd something else to live

The soft and brilliant sleep
the purple haze
the sunshine kind

And Cesare
what was that pain for you
you knew it was a joke
and so did she

You always swore
it is our nakedness that bleeds

At times I hear you in the wall
the blue leech
feeding in your head

And all gifts fall to you
what anger could she lend

Her smile, the way she said
you're dead and were the one
who would not love

The Europe Of The Last has come
it bears your face
and ecstasy is there

DIN OF THE NIGHT

din of the night
on the brick, awakes, thinks

of the peon
in the field, hours hence, muffled
highway, to time sky
in the cockpit, thinks

of his rage in the Berkeley hills
of the room on Noe in summer's choke
of Market's tracks
of her body in lust of
those who pass time
the enlightened, thinks

of the billion
incisions of mind, the heart's
ounce, the ego's insoluble
N-body, *Playboy's*
lady on the bed, baby oil

toilet paper, the snuffed
candle, vaseline, vibrator
waves that flare
miles away, thinks

of the alarm that he rises
to urinate and rose to eat
to count his change
to read of the murders
to go to his work to write
of her hair aflame
under an arm, thinks

in his bare feet, glasses off
the river lights
fuzzed like thistle when
she leaves she is gone, thinks

of the streets, in the acrid light
in amazement, suddenly
in the amazement of it

AS THE SEA SAVES

as the sea saves
rock, continually, as the sea between
all and one—
            why should he be
with any when there is none, New York
palls, he says this now, envoy
of the phobic, cars

drone at the wall, on the loft
bed the girls give
penitence, their call
is life, their busy lives, but
his is wrong, is surely gone
lives now, he says, from week

to week, to the sea said
I won't do anything again, and then
he'd had her in the dream, one
theme, he says, the anger of

one theme, the tide laps
piers, fags loll, ladies
walk with dog, a drag queen on
skates in tulle shoots winks
New Jersey gleams, its song
run for the money, Hugh, art's long

the sky crowds, gulls and scows, busy
life, but gulled to be, in fuck
he fell asleep on her like rock
like an old man, she mocked

him, it was time, having
nothing, say less, but piece it
asswise, tho she refuse
it is as natural as chance—
                              as the sea
who is a woman and seduced

LOVING WOMEN

1   For MM
When I am not with you
it is death and when I am
I am no closer
than the strangers or to you
as what we were
that I never spoke except
of these things
or why were you afraid
to talk to me, in the cockpit,
at the typekeys of the whole sky
and I don't know
why the anger locks
but in the books they know
all day I read *how sick we are*
while the myth wind shrieks
its ax of the present tense
She went with another man
and I call her, Bitch! Whore!
Write: Excuse me. I love you.

54

2   For SN
A strain of blue-eyed Jews
the straight aristocratic nose
and loosely curled
dark brown hair, the real
magazine cover girl,
the shadow
in the photo between M's legs,
the momentary woman off
Central Park, the teenage
nymph in the coach car,
etc., it's done
with mirrors and dildoes, *ben-was*
get a vibrator, right?
and I would have plumbed
in the cold blue of the bedroom
in Mescalito's
fire blue, reaming you, or when I
was the dolphin and sea-fucked
the Sirens of an Odyssey
no man comprehends
or tie me to be whipped
so that my nipples feel
more than pain or smear me
with honey and suck me clean.

3   For BP
It's her ass, excavation
getting nowhere, fast
breasts tipping up and scar

55

where a mole was
sweet and angry
like many and my mammal's
get the woman, otherness of
chill-blooder scaley-pisser's hiss
get to work, the world waits
and don't fail but coldly
in its manner and the rest
like the Buddha, and for love,
and for the women, as I sat-
in on the third floor, the Revolution
when you climbed
from its inside and I pleaded
for the last time
to *come back to me*
at the barricades, in my freedom,
to know they would be beaten
the people
but the Old Man said the personal
runs dry and that renewal was sustenance
was the woods.

4   For BR
In the libraries of universities
yes, that sets me
and somewhere the artists
and the wild girls
who crave them
and those of the barrooms

and everywhere
a slenderness that sets me
unto callowness, the mama warmth
their innocence
less than mine, monstrous
where sciences make
this art obsolete, and oh
I am fine at this
world culture, name droppings,
the 17-year-old's incest, mother
this is what you were
when *I* was a zero, the impetus is
the rhyme was arrived at
without me and I want.

5   For SG
Not a good a time for men, she said
6000 years ago
we broke you
goddesses, burned books,
cut down temples, raped, the rest—
revenge is sweet?
female lips kiss cunt, I too
to come to you
and on the phone the circuit locked
to ring itself
for hours in your room, the sun chime
on the insides of the sky
the hatred of your motherhood,

the overfed, the houses
of anyone, and you
struck as that chime
belonging but an outcast, why
we have found ourselves
and that you have not loved
or will, in your anger,
to goad when I cannot give
the victory or the loss.

6   For LC
In the icelight's view
the buildings of a cold
De Chirico, the last man
alive in his room, people
the mind will not shut
out, I heard
of whom *you* loved, C said
you swore *your* life
a farm, brothers and sisters,
dear friends, so much
warmth I can feel it
on my own cheek even
in this light I can't
alter, and do, in the karma
what might have been as you
got lovely loving me—
that lust towards any
inexhaustible

I understand that awe
as I laughed, little child between
the lost and such law
in the world I have asked
that it bless you.

SECTION 3

DROP THE WIRES

How he thought
he could hold anything

the way a man will hold
what will kill him
unless he had the knack

what my father always said
electricians knew

and they say:
don't touch a dead man
one who has his hands on the wires

and it's not enough to know
you had to
I can hear my father saying

you had to let it go

DEATH, WHICH IS

For LR

Death, which is the climber
the split rope
and the body that the air takes

the clothes ripped
from the intact naked torso

except for the left shoe
except for the broken skull

slung in a leather bag
that they will not let her see

Death, which is the friend
the little cyst, the seed
of rooting in the brain

the eyes unable to see from their sides
and how the body tires but remains
for five slow years

don't drink the alcohol
doctor, when will I die

Death, which is the father
five days before

she saw him dying in the dream
she saw her husband
falling from the tree

and if the husband is the father
and if the mountain is the tree

these things are indelible

Death, which is the woman
drinking the clear cold liquid

drinking the clear cold liquid which is lye

the flesh of the eaten face
the muscles of the stomach
for three weeks alive

And he, who is alive, who hears
these stories of the lives
that buoy like markers

this fix of their existence there
by this, its absence

where he will dream of them
as she had dreamed
as we all must rise up in dreams
to walk among ourselves

THE LAST OR THE FIRST

They were speaking of the sea, the tide's fight
to reap its integrity
the tremble of the plasm seep
deep in
mucous, the throat, sore, clamped on the scream, but

Speaking of the sea, how she sucked
what another rode, choked it and thought
I have not dropped here

It is only that the body knows
defense against ecstasy, cynical, its
jeopardy

      as at any time
without motion of its own
a body might be put

         into jeopardy

Of the sea, of words crumbled
solid on the lips, inexplicable
to her fear
            not out of malice
but the *death* of words, that
they fail us and protect us from
the failure

            to go thru to

the language that arises after it is lost
as they were speaking of, against the sea
or of no sea

The sea

GREENE STREET

It was five and father was home
not of the infinite reaches
but from his labor where the lids fit
and mother had the hammer
saying wait till your father comes

Oh
that was the day when the language worked
when cliches fed the cleaver
from the brotherhood of hooks
and the lion bled and we believed
in the summer that Samson broke

I went on the fire escape of the loft
and saw in a window a woman bent
under the factory's heat
and then turned to your face
having nowhere to turn
from that light that galaxies leave

to the eyes of their art
tho you were not there
nor in the space where I fell
to be alive or dead to be free or caught

AT THE POLE

Those of that dark and their parts
who are drawn to the evil of men

Who came in the dark that was mine
with their hands that work faeces and slime
until I was their art

And I cried God
why am I vile in what is theirs

And why does time humiliate
the time that is before and the time that is after

And why do their tongues elude
to entice me and strike

But what is the answer for those who are forms
when the sun slants
and the creatures cry out for breath

I give them my strength
I live for them
I repeat each road from the dead for them

And then I must speak for them
as an echo speaks
or the blind

Awaking from the sleep where they see

OF THE PLANE

the careless, dishonest in honesty
the clearness of the everywhere
the roaring as distortion, or

power, in repose, the multitudes, the wetness
which is turbulence

at thousands of feet, a deadness like the mind
like thought of
the past for its motion

compression, what all men desire, the possible

the neck bone implored between the lips
the tongue armature certain of the moon

but useless, of no resolution, at the wing struts
equipoise

coming upon, what one flies from, the moment
of propellors, descension

what we are nearer to
inversely, as the sweetness, falsified
the ice hard
odor of the anger

tension & charge, discharge, relaxation

torsion, under the ailerons, inaccessible
pressure, the access
outward to

origin, origin

the broken unending four-stroked
combustible cycle

VERMONT

The energy drain
                into the biologic clock

the power decision of solitude

                Sat Nam

      the Tantrik

the Stones' *Wild Horses*
the "people"
the blank world
& all of my endurance

the unreachable irreducible decimal

        why is this agony maintained

the way is not mine
nor will I climb

75

with Vishnu on his rope
but shut from the pass
in which Nancy stands
against me

who goaded with enlightenment
allegory of Gautama's temptation

child-like or childish

neutral
as the brutal stars

*why are you not
where I am*

Virginia & the twins
beating laundry on the rocks

the all-feeling
wired on the vibes

bugs
logs
cata-
logs

in so far as
I may remember

sentimentality of family warmth
e.g. communes
& drugs don't help, doctor
when we, I, heal myself

                         firefly

Ivan the cat catching mice

                    the mountain set immense
              upon its witness at the dusk

                    the radiant list
              of the billions in breath

         to the key of the bee
                    in the locks of the field

              the machine that is not machine

thus Jeans reminded
mind is matter

space-time's
weld without seam

                    entrance
seconds of transcendence

                    our family tree
            in the back country's
                                    vanguard

the lintels of the door

one end of the sky
to the other
& again

            we walk

                    cloud on sun
            devastation of puberty

                                    arms implored
                        to the rain mother

                smoldering

anger
            unreasoned & unappeasable
                                    the steel

                            indictment
                        windlass
                                    creak of the tree
                        torrent forest

                            78

                            light
            asunder at the sky-crack
                                    my own

                        deceptions
                                    cracked
asunder

            on the road
                        & then hell fell
                                    the house

                fire dryness

Xrist too got off
Reich will get you there
feel bad but feel

coherence

grinning neighbor: T'ai Ch'i master bearing
huge purple flower

                    come join us to chant
                    the sun in

Nancy I accused you of arrogance
your barbed insistence

alive to another's pain
but not in pity or seduction

motionlessness

buttercup
in the flange
of the road

Kundalini's burst
thru the crown chakra's lotus

penis erect
in REM sleep's fragment

suck & kiss of the clover

jail terminus

the terror of descent

my father's battles
in the bars of the city

in the orgone's great
circle of return

these first artisans

SECTION 4

STORY

Ill & dying:
who would persuade him he was not?
Technique. It was pure technique.
The woman squeezing back the child,
denying the possible pleasure.
He was too tired to argue.
It was like lifting a weight.
He was sitting then,
finally, on the red steps.
The doctor had given him the pills.
He was distant, not himself.
The conversations grated.
He did not enjoy these people.
He did not . . .
He was sitting on the red steps.
The children were behind him in the house.
A woman in a blue dress
was visible thru the trees.
His mouth was dry—the pills.
He knew it would never stop.

He heard them splashing in the pool.
Some in swim suits.
Some in underwear.
A girl's wet jersey
matted on her breasts.
He turned his face away.
A dog whined.
A child ran naked from the edge.
Someone covered her with a towel.
Lips blue and trembling.
He finished his drink.
He looked at the other side.
A woman was pouring chlorine,
cleansing the detritus
the swimmers had introduced.

WHY IMMANUEL CAN'T

Chain level had been found
buildings hugged ground
in their righteousness, sun's face
machined on their edges
this is the solitude the fly
hummed on its leg
but in the world again
the lathes were thinking children
it was a hard life for the hands
and nothing deterred them not
their lunge for dispassion
nor their song below the quanta
streaming out like scars
the axiom
of the mind as one and of the anger
at what the mind is not, the foot
kicking rock against
duality of the eye alone
as the Chinaman who wound
the glass frog

dreaming of its fall
in the gravity of hurt's null slamming
tonnage to a steel
blood drilled and mocking
cadence to the heart

SCREEN DREAM

At her inversely as the stars are
said to recede the gesture is
to turn away the face repeated
as the stars are unreasoning
as death's hand to masturbate
the unhealed cold as space

The pain is not intense enough
called clarity as I ached
for my dead sister
tho I had no sister
and finally for the first time
the machine gun riddled me
playing dead I was dead
contorted to escape the inescap-
able spurt of light and evil

A man among the women works
domestic made substance
that consoles no longer

tho it was the true flesh
now acid of the blood blond
mandala's milk drop and nipple
voluptuous as Barbara her
esoteric philosophic mind
unbelievable

And I have no illusions this year
for the moon is my death mask
and what beckons me is bone
when the day force runs least
to she who is pig slitter utterly
tender and terrible at rush
of his nakedness as men hack
the skin they are

BARBARA'S ORIGEN

Chains and bodily torture
agony in iron and the darkness of his cell
threats of the fire and torment
slowly and with care as instructed
that he not be permitted
to die beneath their hands
admonishing himself to the glory of martyrdom
the ecstasy of fasting and castration
etc.

If the origin fits, infecting me
on the Cape your breasts
had atoned me to sanctity
years, as I have always been
entrapped to return to you, his heat
at us that first hour
transfigured to your face
and it did not leave you

If the natural needs nothing
and if only the offenses want words

my relation to him
will not be the fault of our similar grace
and I will not assign you
to his torturers or torture
but note that it is so
and not of my invention
in the constant invention
to which you had been lost and offered

SHUNTING IN

Drum of the voltage count
fifth dimensional quantum arc
who on the planet is high enough
heart's step-
up transformer scaled out of brain jam
Orpheus tuned to the grid & I felt
pure father current
shorted thru pelvis, the past's
amperage of image at
thigh's high tension line
grounded to cunt & strung
to the astral capacitor's
violet crackling discharge
charring at both ends of nakedness

Tangible spider steeled electric
generation of her prison
years fusing switches, the ion flow
thru the sweat of a solitude
the power sea shoring charging

Hephaestus the clangorer & crippled
to the lightning of that Venus
churinga & lingam
thru the vacuum & resistance as when
my father's heartbeat failed
one in three & wired
to the cathode tube he beamed
to see Susan, a dead man's touch
shooting sparks from fingertips
magnetic for a girl's eyes
the dark bloody turbines
the mausoleums & the moistness

AUBADE

a nostalgia of the dawn's mirror
mythic as the past where we poised
in its signal for the hands
to accept as the glass accepts all vigils
tho it is clear how I had held you
at the fissure that was face
that saw but would not sanctify
and in the cell under the lamps
where men are sold
for your necklace and its teeth
your lead eyes heated bones to transparence
and the indecipherable glyph of a hair
cracked on the sink
as the stars sparked to give witness
and there was no humility, no humbleness

THE BUS TREADS 10TH

The bus treads 10th, the riders
climb, it's late, I'm up
to see you as you are, the night
seeps in, the fear, for weeks
I tense against the hands, I hear
the couples curse, the cat jumps
to the floor, the doors
of smoke, the doors, he flicks
a blade against its spring
this is not I, tho I am he
the poem begins
another war, you are
so beautiful she said, their soles
tap down the hall, it's fall
again, we cling, this bus runs
straight and soon, my god
is this your room, the TV shines
like Buddha and his crown

the walls are brown, their axes
hack the door, they know
this note, this time, this moon
and now it's we who dance

PERSEPHONE

Brown hair dyed red
forged passport to Havana, forced
free comrade love to break

Patriarch's middle class, cancerous
mother of the politic, brutal
child, opening, silver of night

bloom in the subways, gunning, air
robbed in the fluorescence, you
could feel her unbalance

scales, sun nowhere, tho in her
at the Power Drain's insane coin
her blood hole, tattoo, a queen's

sign of the day-force at its failure
nipple of mandala, Death's muse
or why write what is reduced to

a fecal gold, a Midas walled
in the rectal crypts, befouled
Kundalini snake of slime twined

in the fig tree as tracks gorge
the earth's bowel to tell time
on the toilet train's pure form

as it is the underworld, darling
on the elevator in fur with her one-headed
dogs, nights in Hell's field

the lights burn dark in dark time
in the bars where she is art among
true crime, in thigh boots, white

lipped, worms are alive on her, the wings
of her hips beat where men kill tho
I don't die but squeeze

impotence and rage to send them
to her hands where the cars roar
as I roared for the toy sword

she would not buy in her rings
intractable, in bracelets, in fragrances
mocker of men, awaking me

MUSE

She is always right
this is a work of privilege
of great pride and privilege

He will forget himself, he says
but in the street he hunted her
in their city there is too much law

They abound and are never women
tho it is a privilege to let them be
lovely as money

As S said, there are parts of the heart
that are entirely dead
there is the way called ecstasy

She walked the block
tho he did not show attendance
he followed but did not approach

The petulant head turned like the hundreds
who are nameless to vanity
he watched her as was his privilege

The rage beats him to disgrace
humiliates him tho he eats of it
passionate for endurance

His parents ask of romance
his hands cramp at the type
his arms tense, confession, confession

He increments but is motionless
the rigid stamen shoots
to have it crack him, crack him down

Let him curse when it is felt
let him spit at the master
who makes marriage to this mistress

He is forfeit to her service
inescapable for she is proven—
out of nothing, nothing

One week he wedged on the bed
uroboros, saw no one, the cars sped
he did not beg her

The lit forms jumped in the dark
it was his life in the pith
projected tho he could not stop

Tracked on her wheel into utterance
moving as it moved, stripped
and grown monstrous from its word

Lord, let him live

SECTION 5

UNTOWARDS

he is the pig his mother dreamed
the cancerous fairy with the bloody stool the filth
they were hiding in the houses of the grave the beautiful

as syphilis is set in the ultraviolet photo
or the knife scar with its whiteness on the thigh
no different than the laughable and taking it

as the rest have taken it sweating at the armpits
kissing the tight lipped murderers who wait
for the false face that is always at the curb

at six P.M. the alcohol cool day in the maul of summer
the accidental air striking his cheek
the trilling of orgone in the rooms of the universe

far far from him but there if he would enter
rise from his agony to feel that to feel was the work
in the life that writes itself at the pun beyond artfulness

the solace of the hands on the body of one who is loved
but where he asks where is this sustenance
as the sun wind to bare him again and by accident

AT LIBERATION

Embolus
boiling in the mind
as the woman came
to that light smeared
at the windows
like a pus to photograph
the women as he sat
alone in his room
in that light that they
entered on the film
transformed
as he was not

In the dream
they are milk of the moon
yet here is the hairy lip
the profane mouth of blood
the budding
tongue of rage heated
in the spider's acid

that logos spilled
female in the city
in the courtship culture
in their time to take
hate to heart, myth
that they make to become

It hooks
in the catch of his eye
each glint and gate
of their space he skirts
like a desert or ice
in fear of them
or on that film
where it vibrates
stolen or lost
from their past that he aches
to return to, to work
as in the flesh
that they shut from him
to assume their flesh

POEM

A father's coins, his belt buckle
shining like a tooth, suspenders
twitching buttons from the mama box
underwear lint, garter belts, Modess
that a boy bought, the electroshock
calling like a phone, all years
from her white hair and I hate him
who burned her in that scaffold
that steel rocket bed
he must have been a great maniac
thundering his bolts but curse
all fathers they are not mine
there is no mother who scrubbed
while sisters danced, no photographs
I break all as she broke, I forget
I kill the ant for bad karma
and I don't care, I am
bastard and born at last

JOURNAL

Forefinger at anus goading the years
Clenched in skin at diaphragm as energy centered
Karate kata flash of great succulent red fleshed cock bidding me
                                        suck brought tears
Hatred after loss of you made others unenterable
Tense head moved of its own accord
Eyes took slits as light hurt
Jerked myself hard for you for exhaustion
Laughed about letting the body alone to learn itself
Saw you were no mother mesh no comforter but emptiness and no one
Screamed out lack and to save myself from lack had I known
Clamped for weeks awaiting a solution
Old saying said: *there* is the door and its use

UNDER THE FLOOR

The way a man wedged in under the floor
will hear the footfalls of the others
treading on the boards

will hear their tapping at the mark
and will believe they are the searchers

where he lies
pressed against the bottom of their soles
or with eye upon the faces of their clocks
in those hours below the cracks

when the shoes unlace and drop upon his heart
and his scrapings are the noise
before the mind awakes

to move that nail
that scratches on his eyelid, the unchanged

where the boards creak and he remembers
why he does not sleep
while the silent pulse drums in the inlay

for there he has become the floor
from which men arise and are pulled toward

CLEAR LIGHT

Clear light not of reason, sham
of thought to choke its reason, work
love and know—what purpose ego-loss
nirvana and the wheel are one

From the plane I saw orgone's play
north lights of the Buddha
the acetylene of his crown tho why name
what is nameless, no man cuts the root
tho the mind grind each sick cell

In the past I made the brain
be the money of shit, parasite
so gross it eats itself to be served
by men sold for the whore of its cake

Tits gone, cunt sown, fag put-on
fucked by what beats them, mock lambs
butchered at the bank, comedians
clipping coupons in arboreal dells
still swilling rot-gut

110

Lips snickering in the mouths
of the pig celebrities, in the skinny
clothes model's crotch, as E said
how we loathe her yet are
insanely drawn, the world's cohesion

Body racked in the black wind
a squid starving in its ink
as in the spring when it hates
that fire of the air, maniacal to kill
that day that J spoke of him who dug
out his genitals with his nails

Of the cracked vase that healed
in his dream, that a form could
heal as the vision broke and lit me
and broke as quickly as the sun breaks
to be dark tho its gases lash
and flare upon a hundred million miles

THE ARTISTS

Of course it is only
another day, the first in eternity
the shadow of the gallows
of course they care nothing for the work
the pictures of a God
on the walls of the slaughterhouse
the blood backdrops
impassive in their rightness

Lord
I went on the earth from these craftsmen
it was an age to mason flesh
I sat in their hell myth
from which none have arisen
I discovered myself
in the service of a form that had outlived me
the white noise that darkness knows oh
they know how the pigment is a blow
how much bone to the blood
how much ardor for the hardness

they are gentle
to the screams the wheels under oil
slashing steel they think
to change this into gold

Oh Lord
I begged you to break me of bitterness
I lowered my arms
in the gears and they ground me
it meant
nothing
I know how the blade slides in
the cross on the belly I feel
the pleasure when the brush is dipped
I understand the certainty
that one is clear
that they would pay
but I swear to you
not even death there was yours
and the stones
were being hammered to believe